The Ultimate Dad Jokes Book for Kids

600 Clean, Lighthearted, Hilarious yet Cringe Worthy Jokes for Kids and the Whole Family!

© **Copyright 2024** - All rights reserved. The contents of this book may not be reproduced, duplicated or transmitted without direct written permission from the author. Under no circumstances will any legal responsibility or blame be held against the publisher for any reparation, damages, or monetary loss due to the information herein, either directly or indirectly.

Legal Notice: This book is copyright protected. This is only for personal use. You cannot amend, distribute, sell, use, quote or paraphrase any part or the content within this book without the consent of the author.

Disclaimer Notice: Please note the information contained within this document is for educational and entertainment purposes only. Every attempt has been made to provide accurate, up to date and reliable complete information. No warranties of any kind are expressed or implied. Readers acknowledge that the author is not engaging in the rendering of legal, financial, medical or professional advice. The content of this book has been derived from various sources. Please consult a licensed professional before attempting any techniques outlined in this book. By reading this document, the reader agrees that under no circumstances is the author responsible for any losses, direct or indirect, which are incurred as a result of the use of information contained within this document, including, but not limited to, errors, omissions, or inaccuracies.

Dedication

To my two amazing daughters,
Sophia and Holly—
Thank you for always laughing at my
jokes... even when you didn't get them (or
pretended you didn't). You've made being a
dad the most excellent punchline of all.
This one's for you—whether you like it or
not!
Love, Daddy

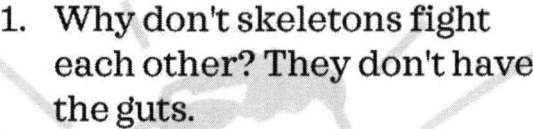

1. Why don't skeletons fight each other? They don't have the guts.

2. What do you call fake spaghetti? An impasta.

3. Why did the scarecrow win an award? He was outstanding in his field.

4. How do you organize a space party? You planet.

5. Why did the math book look sad? It had too many problems.

6. Why don't eggs tell jokes? They'd crack each other up.

7. What do you call cheese that isn't yours? Nacho cheese.

8. Why couldn't the bicycle stand up by itself? It was two-tired.

9. How do you make a tissue dance? You put a little boogie in it.

10. What do you call a fish wearing a crown? A kingfish.

11. Why did the tomato turn red? Because it saw the salad dressing.

12. What did one wall say to the other wall? I'll meet you at the corner.

13. Why don't oysters share their pearls? Because they're shellfish.

14. What do you call a can opener that doesn't work? A can't opener.

15. How do you catch a squirrel? Climb a tree and act like a nut.

16. What did the ocean say to the beach? Nothing, it just waved.

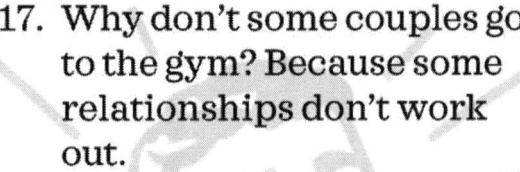

17. Why don't some couples go to the gym? Because some relationships don't work out.

18. What kind of shoes do ninjas wear? Sneakers.

19. What did one traffic light say to the other? "Stop looking, I'm changing!"

20. What do you call a bear with no teeth? A gummy bear.

21. Why was the belt arrested? It held up a pair of pants.

22. What do you call a sleeping bull? A bulldozer.

23. Why did the golfer bring two pairs of pants? In case he got a hole in one.

24. How does a penguin build its house? Igloos it together.

25. Why don't skeletons fight? They don't have the backbone.

26. What do you get if you cross a snowman and a vampire? Frostbite.

27. How do cows stay up to date? They read the moos-paper.

28. What do you call a cow with no legs? Ground beef.

29. Why did the cookie go to the doctor? Because it felt crumby.

30. Why was the broom so good at its job? It swept everyone off their feet.

31. Why was the broom late? It swept in.

32. How does a train eat? It goes chew chew!

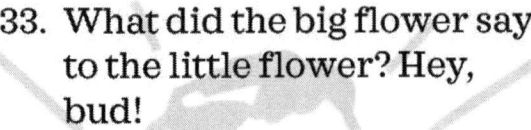

33. What did the big flower say to the little flower? Hey, bud!

34. Why did the picture go to jail? It was framed.

35. Why did the stadium get hot after the game? All the fans left.

36. What kind of tree fits in your hand? A palm tree.

37. Why did the banana go to the doctor? It wasn't peeling well.

38. How do you make holy water? You boil the hell out of it.

39. What do you call a pencil with two erasers? Pointless.

40. Why was the computer cold? It left its Windows open.

41. How do you fix a cracked pumpkin? With a pumpkin patch.

42. Why can't your nose be 12 inches long? Because then it would be a foot.

43. What did the janitor say when he jumped out of the closet? Supplies!

44. Why did the fish blush? Because it saw the ocean's bottom.

45. What kind of music do mummies listen to? Wrap music.

46. Why don't you ever see elephants hiding in trees? Because they're so good at it.

47. What do you call a factory that makes good products? A satisfactory.

48. How does a cucumber become a pickle? It goes through a jarring experience.

49. Why are elevator jokes so good? Because they work on so many levels.

50. What did the grape do when it got stepped on? Nothing, it just let out a little wine.

51. Why don't skeletons ever go trick or treating? Because they have no body to go with.

52. What do you call a singing computer? A Dell.

53. Why don't some fish play piano? Because you can't tuna fish.

54. What do you call a factory that makes just OK products? A medi-ocre.

55. Why did the coffee file a police report? It got mugged.

56. Why did the computer go to the doctor? Because it had a virus.

57. What do you call a snowman with a six-pack? An abdominal snowman.

58. Why are frogs so happy? They eat whatever bugs them.

59. Why do seagulls fly over the sea? Because if they flew over the bay, they'd be bagels.

60. What do you call a deer with no eyes? No idea.

61. How do you keep a bull from charging? Take away its credit card.

62. What did one plate say to the other plate? Lunch is on me.

63. What do you call an alligator in a vest? An investigator.

64. Why do cows wear bells? Because their horns don't work.

65. Why do bees hum? Because they don't know the words.

66. Why did the chicken join a band? Because it had the drumsticks.

67. What do you call a pile of cats? A meowtain.

68. What did one hat say to the other? Stay here, I'm going on ahead.

69. Why are ghosts such bad liars? Because you can see right through them.

70. What's orange and sounds like a parrot? A carrot.

71. Why don't melons get married? Because they cantaloupe.

72. How does a snowman get around? By riding an "icicle."

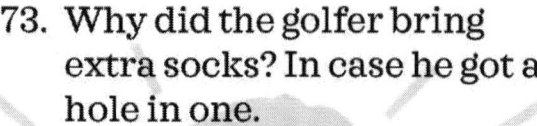

73. Why did the golfer bring extra socks? In case he got a hole in one.

74. What did the buffalo say when his son left for college? Bison.

75. Why did the man put his money in the blender? Because he wanted to make some liquid assets.

76. How does a lion like his steak? Medium roar.

77. What do you call a dog magician? A labracadabrador.

78. Why are ghosts bad liars? Because they are too transparent.

79. Why don't skeletons ever go to parties? Because they have no body to dance with.

80. What do you call a pig that does karate? A pork chop.

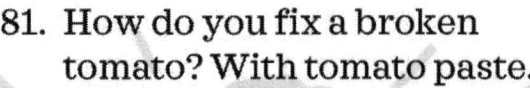

81. How do you fix a broken tomato? With tomato paste.

82. Why did the toilet paper roll down the hill? To get to the bottom.

83. What do you call a cow that plays an instrument? A moosician.

84. How does a vampire start a letter? Tomb it may concern.

85. What did one eye say to the other eye? Between you and me, something smells.

86. What do you call a belt made of watches? A waist of time.

87. Why don't football players play hide and seek? They'd never get past the goal.

88. What do you call a lazy kangaroo? A pouch potato.

89. Why did the broom stay late? It had to sweep up.

90. How do you make a lemon drop? Just let it fall.

91. What did one elevator say to the other? I think I'm coming down with something.

92. Why do elephants never use computers? They're afraid of the mouse.

93. What's brown and sticky? A stick.

94. Why did the bike fall over? Because it was two-tired.

95. What do you call a cat that can sing? A meowsician.

96. Why did the man put his money in the blender? He wanted to make some liquid assets.

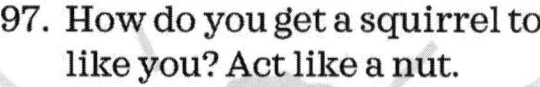

97. How do you get a squirrel to like you? Act like a nut.

98. What did the grape do when it was stepped on? It let out a little wine.

99. Why don't scientists trust atoms? Because they make up everything.

100. What's the best way to watch a fly fishing tournament? Live stream.

101. Why did the mushroom go to the party alone? Because he's a fungi.

102. What do you call a bee that can't make up its mind? A maybe.

103. How do you catch a whole school of fish? With bookworms.

104. Why was the baby strawberry crying? Because its parents were in a jam.

105. What did the left eye say to the right eye? Between us, something smells.

106. Why did the basketball team go to the bank? They wanted to get their bounce checked.

107. What do you call a snake wearing a hard hat? A boa constructor.

108. What did the toaster say to the bread? "I'm on a roll!"

109. Why are spiders great baseball players? Because they know how to catch flies.

110. What did the big chimney say to the little chimney? You're too young to smoke.

111. Why don't skeletons play music in church? They have no organs.

112. What did the grape say to the blueberry? "Breathe, buddy, breathe!"

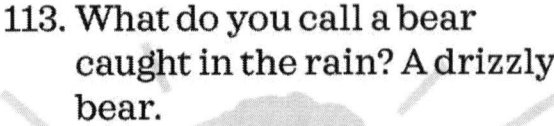

113. What do you call a bear caught in the rain? A drizzly bear.

114. Why did the dog sit in the shade? It didn't want to be a hot dog.

115. Why don't you ever see elephants hiding in trees? Because they're so good at it.

116. What do you call a fish with no eyes? Fsh.

117. What do you call a nervous javelin thrower? Shakespeare.

118. What did one snowman say to the other snowman? Do you smell carrots?

119. Why do cows have hooves instead of feet? Because they lactose.

120. What kind of shoes do frogs wear? Open toad sandals.

121. How do you find Will Smith in the snow? Look for fresh prints.

122. What's blue and smells like red paint? Blue paint.

123. Why was the big cat disqualified from the race? Because it was a cheetah.

124. Why don't you ever see hippopotamuses hiding in trees? Because they're really good at it.

125. What do you call a snobby criminal walking downstairs? A con descending.

126. What do you call a fish that wears a crown? A kingfish.

127. What kind of room doesn't have doors? A mushroom.

128. Why was the sand wet? Because the seaweed.

129. How do you know the ocean is friendly? It waves.

130. Why can't you hear a pterodactyl in the bathroom? Because it has a silent pee.

131. What do you call a dinosaur with an extensive vocabulary? A thesaurus.

132. Why don't koalas count as bears? They don't have the right koalafications.

133. What do you call a belt with a watch on it? A waist of time.

134. Why did the scarecrow win an award? Because he was outstanding in his field.

135. What do you call a dinosaur that's sleeping? A dino-snore.

136. Why did the cow break up with the farmer? It found someone more a-moos-ing.

137. What kind of music do planets like? Neptunes.

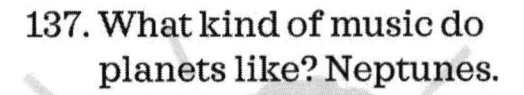

138. What do you get when you cross a snowman with a vampire? Frostbite.

139. How does a vampire start a letter? "Tomb it may concern."

140. Why don't sharks like fast food? Because they can't catch it.

141. What did the big flower say to the little flower? Hi, bud!

142. Why don't skeletons go to parties? Because they have no body to dance with.

143. What's a bird's favorite type of math? Owl-gebra.

144. How does the Easter Bunny stay in shape? He eggs-ercises!

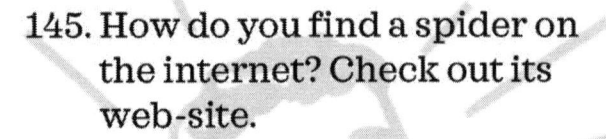

145. How do you find a spider on the internet? Check out its web-site.

146. How do porcupines hug? Very carefully.

147. Why did the bicycle fall over? It was two-tired.

148. Why don't skeletons fight? They don't have the guts.

149. Why don't oysters share their pearls? Because they're shellfish.

150. What did one wall say to the other wall? I'll meet you at the corner.

151. What do you get when you cross a snowman and a vampire? Frostbite.

152. Why did the cookie go to the doctor? Because it was feeling crummy.

153. What did the grape do when it got stepped on? It let out a little wine.

154. Why don't you ever see elephants hiding in trees? Because they're really good at it.

155. How does the moon cut its hair? Eclipse it.

156. Did you hear about the circus fire? It was in tents.

157. What did the fish say when it swam into a wall? Dam.

158. Why can't you give Elsa a balloon? Because she'll let it go.

159. What did one hat say to the other hat? You stay here, I'll go on ahead.

160. How do you catch a unique rabbit? Unique up on it.

161. Why did the math book look so sad? Because it had too many problems.

162. I'm reading a book on anti-gravity. It's impossible to put down!

163. Why was the stadium so hot after the game? All the fans left.

164. Parallel lines have so much in common. It's a shame they'll never meet.

165. Why don't scientists trust atoms? Because they make up everything!

166. Want to hear a joke about construction? I'm still working on it.

167. Did you hear about the guy who invented Lifesavers? He made a mint!

168. Why can't you hear a pterodactyl go to the bathroom? Because the "P" is silent.

169. I told my wife she was drawing her eyebrows too high. She looked surprised.

170. Why are fish so smart? Because they live in schools.

171. Did you hear the one about the roof? Never mind, it's over your head.

172. I used to play piano by ear, but now I use my hands.

173. What did one ocean say to the other ocean? Nothing, they just waved.

174. Why did the tomato turn red? Because it saw the salad dressing!

175. Want to hear a joke about a piece of paper? Never mind, it's tearable.

176. I would avoid the sushi if I was you. It's a little fishy.

177. Did you hear about the cheese factory explosion? There was nothing left but de-brie.

178. Why was the calendar always so popular? It had a lot of dates.

179. What kind of car does a sheep like to drive? A lamborghini.

180. I don't trust stairs. They're always up to something.

181. Why do we never see elephants hiding in trees? Because they're so good at it.

182. I told my friend 10 jokes to make him laugh. Sadly, no pun in ten did.

183. I only know 25 letters of the alphabet. I don't know y.

184. I'm on a seafood diet. I see food and I eat it. It's not working out well.

185. I once got into a fight with a broken elevator. I took it to another level.

186. I'd tell you a joke about an elevator, but it's an uplifting experience.

187. The only time I set the bar low is when I'm cleaning the floor.

188. I tried to catch some fog earlier. I mist.

189. I used to be a baker, but I couldn't make enough dough.

190. I'm reading a book about anti-gravity. It's impossible to put down.

191. I told my doctor I wanted to be cremated. She made an appointment for next Tuesday.

192. What did the fisherman say to the magician? "Pick a cod, any cod!"

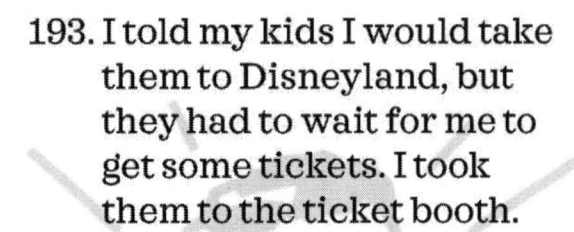

193. I told my kids I would take them to Disneyland, but they had to wait for me to get some tickets. I took them to the ticket booth.

194. I went to buy some camo pants but couldn't find any.

195. I'm afraid for the calendar. Its days are numbered.

196. I once asked a librarian if the library had any books on paranoia. She whispered, "They're right behind you."

197. I have a split personality," said Tom, being Frank.

198. I couldn't figure out how to put my seatbelt on. Then it "clicked"!

199. What do you get when you cross a snowman with a dog? Frostbite.

200. I'm writing a book on reverse psychology. Please don't buy it.

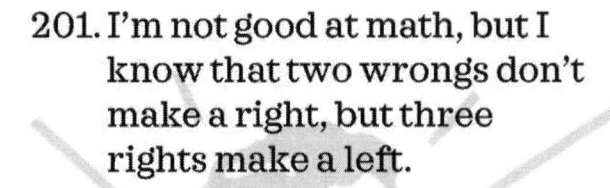

201. I'm not good at math, but I know that two wrongs don't make a right, but three rights make a left.

202. I told my wife she should embrace her mistakes. She gave me a hug.

203. I would avoid the sushi if I were you. It's a little fishy.

204. I told my computer I needed a break, and now it won't stop sending me beach photos.

205. My friend says to me, "What rhymes with orange?" I said, "No it doesn't!"

206. I joined a gym and I have a new plan. I'm going to train my muscles to get bigger by lifting my spirits.

207. Why don't skeletons go to parties? They have no body to go with.

208. I threw a boomerang and now I'm living in constant fear.

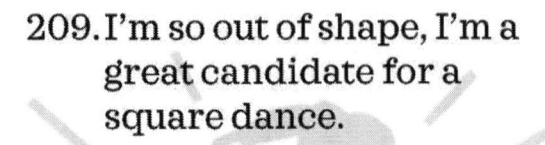

209. I'm so out of shape, I'm a great candidate for a square dance.

210. I once knew a guy who was addicted to brake fluid. He says he can stop anytime.

211. My wife told me to stop impersonating a flamingo. I had to put my foot down.

212. I'm not great at cooking. The smoke alarm is my sous-chef.

213. I took my wife's advice and started jogging. Now I'm halfway to the fridge and back.

214. I spilled spot remover on my dog. Now he's gone.

215. I told my doctor I broke my arm in two places. He told me to stop going to those places.

216. Why did the scientist bring a ladder to the lab? To reach new heights.

217. I wanted to be a banker, but I lost interest.

218. I bought a new bed but now I'm having trouble sleeping. It's like I'm "over-sleeping" on it.

219. I'm really good at my job at the orange juice factory, but my boss says I lack concentration.

220. Why do ducks have feathers? To cover their butt quacks.

221. I once tried to be a carpenter, but my work was just a "plank" in the road to success.

222. What do you call a fish without eyes? Fsh.

223. I gave up my seat at the bar for a man who lost his balance. Now he's back and I'm stuck standing.

224. I'm so good at my job, they gave me a raise – but I had to keep my old salary for training.

225. How does a lion like his steak? Medium rare.

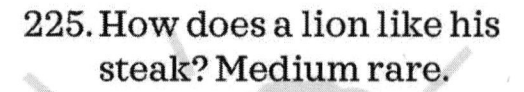

226. I went to buy some camo pants, but couldn't find any. Guess I need to improve my "hide-and-seek" skills.

227. What did the left eye say to the right eye? Between you and me, something smells.

228. Why did the sandwich go to the beach? It needed a little sand-wich.

229. I told my kids I'd help them with their homework if they did the same for me. Now I'm "homework" with a few questions of my own.

230. I asked the librarian if the library had any books on paranoia. She said they're right behind me.

231. I went to the zoo and saw a gorilla reading a book. The zookeeper said it was a "read-bait."

232. I asked the trainer at the gym how to lose weight. He said, "Don't eat it."

233. I'm so bad at fishing, I've become an expert at using worms as bait.

234. I once tried to be a gardener, but my plants just wouldn't "grow" on me.

235. Why don't oysters donate to charity? Because they're shellfish.

236. I had to sell my vacuum cleaner. It was just gathering dust.

237. I'm not a great cook. My microwave has more recipes than I do.

238. I went to the beach and found a "sand-tastic" treasure. It was just a bunch of seashells - a real "beach" day.

239. I gave up my job as a banker for a career in music. It's a bit of a "note-worthy" change.

240. I'm so bad at math, I can't even count on myself.

241. I tried to be a magician but gave up. I just couldn't make the "disappearing" act work.

242. I got a haircut today. The barber said it was "incredible" – now I'm questioning his taste.

243. I'm on a whiskey diet. I've lost three days already.

244. I tried to be a gardener, but my plants just wouldn't "grow" on me.

245. How does a cow stay up to date? It subscribes to the moo-s-paper.

246. I tried to join a gym, but I couldn't "lift" my spirits to go.

247. I'm not great with technology. I'm still trying to "sync" my old-school VHS tapes.

248. I wanted to be a stand-up comedian, but my jokes fell flat. Now I'm just sitting down.

249. I thought I saw a spider in the bath, but it was just a "web" of lies.

250. I'm terrible at tennis. My serves are so bad, they're always "faulty."

251. I told my wife I'd give up smoking, but that's a pipe dream.

252. Why did the scarecrow become a successful neurosurgeon? Because he was outstanding in his field.

253. Why did the bicycle need a nap? It was two-tired.

254. Why did the frog sit on the lily pad? Because it didn't want to croak too soon.

255. I used to be a librarian, but it was just a novel idea.

256. What's the best way to carve wood? Whittle by whittle.

257. I told my wife I'm going to start a band. She said, "Are you serious?" I said, "No, I'm just joking."

258. I told my friend ten jokes to make him laugh. Sadly, no pun in ten did.

259. I'm on a seafood diet. I see food and I eat it.

260. What did the grape do when he got stepped on? Nothing but let out a little wine!

261. I'm reading a book on reverse psychology. Please don't buy it.

262. I told my kids I'd take them to Disneyland, but they had to wait for me to get some tickets. I took them to the ticket booth.

263. I'm not great at math, but I know that two wrongs don't make a right, but three rights make a left.

264. I used to be a banker, but I lost interest.

265. I told my wife I'm reading a book on anti-gravity. It's impossible to put down.

266. Why was the pirate bad at cooking? He couldn't get his sea legs.

267. What did the ocean say to the shore? Nothing, it just waved.

268. I'm terrible at telling time. I always say the second hand first.

269. I'm so bad at fishing, I've become an expert at catching nothing.

270. I threw a boomerang years ago; now I live in constant fear.

271. I'm reading a book on glue. I just can't put it down.

272. What's a skeleton's least favorite room? The living room.

273. Why don't vampires take selfies? They don't show up in pictures.

274. Why did the scarecrow win an award? He was outstanding in his field!

275. What kind of dog loves to take bubble baths? A shampoo-dle.

276. What did the grape do when it got stepped on? Nothing, it just let out a little wine!

277. What did one wall say to the other? "Meet you at the corner!"

278. How do cows stay up to date with the news? They read the moos-paper!

279. I told my dog a joke about fetching, but he just didn't get it.

280. Why don't some fish play basketball? They're afraid of the net.

281. What did the judge say when the skunk entered the courtroom? "Odor in the court!"

282. Why do seagulls fly over the ocean? Because if they flew over the bay, they'd be bagels!

283. Why don't vampires have any friends? They're a pain in the neck.

284. Why don't leopards play hide and seek? Because they're always spotted.

285. I only know how to tell dad jokes... I guess it's a fathomable skill.

286. What did the fish say when it hit the wall? "Dam."

287. I made a pencil with two erasers... It was pointless!

288. What did the janitor say when he jumped out of the closet? "Supplies!"

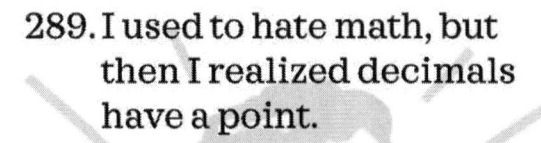

289. I used to hate math, but then I realized decimals have a point.

290. Did you hear about the bakery that burned down? Their business is toast.

291. What did the toilet say to the other toilet? "You look flushed."

292. How do trees get online? They log in.

293. What do you call a sleeping bull? A bulldozer!

294. Why did the tomato blush? Because it saw the salad dressing!

295. What's a tornado's favorite game? Twister.

296. Why do bananas never get lonely? Because they hang out in bunches.

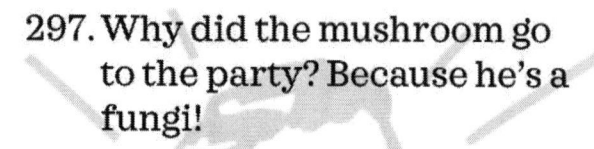

297. Why did the mushroom go to the party? Because he's a fungi!

298. How do you know when the moon has had enough to eat? It's full.

299. What's a vampire's least favorite food? Steak.

300. I wanted to take pictures of fog, but I mist my chance.

301. I gave my friend an apple pie. She said it was so good, it was un-peel-ievable.

302. Why are fish so smart? Because they live in schools.

303. Did you hear about the kidnapping at school? Don't worry, he woke up.

304. Why can't you give Elsa a balloon? She'll let it go.

305. I went to a seafood disco last week. Pulled a mussel.

306. Why did the student eat his homework? Because the teacher said it was a piece of cake!

307. I tried to start a hide-and-seek club, but it didn't work out. Good players are hard to find.

308. Why did the cookie go to the doctor? It was feeling crummy.

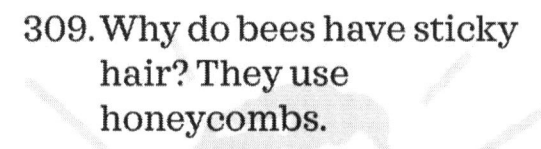

309. Why do bees have sticky hair? They use honeycombs.

310. What did one plate say to the other? Lunch is on me.

311. Why are frogs so happy? Because they eat whatever bugs them.

312. What did the janitor say after a big mess? "This is mop-tastic!"

313. I used to be addicted to the hokey pokey, but I turned myself around.

314. Why do ducks have feathers? To cover their butt-quacks.

315. Why don't you see giraffes in elementary school? Because they're all in high school!

316. I went to buy some camouflage pants, but I couldn't find any.

317. What did one snowman say to the other? "Do you smell carrots?"

318. Why don't ants get sick? They have tiny ant-bodies.

319. Why do math teachers love parks? Because of all the natural logs.

320. How do you find Will Smith in the snow? You look for fresh prints.

321. Why did the teddy bear say no to dessert? Because it was already stuffed.

322. Why was the stadium so cool? It was full of fans.

323. What did the big flower say to the little flower? "Hey, bud!"

324. How does a cow stay up to date? It follows the moos!

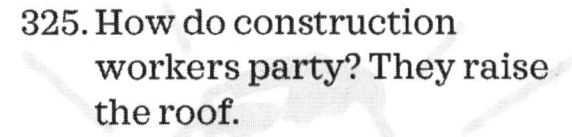

325. How do construction workers party? They raise the roof.

326. I told a joke about a roof, but it went over your head.

327. I wanted to learn to juggle, but I couldn't keep all the balls in the air.

328. Why are elevator jokes so good? They're uplifting.

329. Why was the broom always tired? It was always sweeping!

330. I bought a belt made entirely of watches. It was a waist of time.

331. What do you call a dinosaur that crashes his car? Tyrannosaurus wrecks.

332. Why did the dog sit in the shade? Because he didn't want to be a hot dog.

333. Why can't you give a balloon to a porcupine? It'll pop!

334. Why do birds fly south for the winter? Because it's too far to walk.

335. How do you stop a bull from charging? Take away its credit card.

336. Why are skeletons so calm? Because nothing gets under their skin.

337. What did one eye say to the other eye? "Between you and me, something smells."

338. Why don't sharks eat clowns? They taste funny.

339. Why did the math teacher go to the beach? She needed some sine and cosine.

340. What did the buffalo say to his son when he dropped him off at school? Bison.

341. What's a cat's favorite color? Purrr-ple!

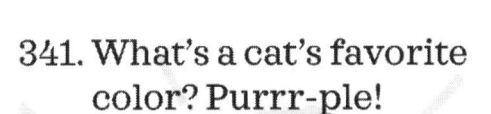

342. What did the frog order at the fast-food restaurant? French flies and a diet croak.

343. Why did the teddy bear say no to dessert? Because it was stuffed.

344. What did the tree say to the wind? "Leaf me alone!"

345. I opened a bakery, but business is crumby.

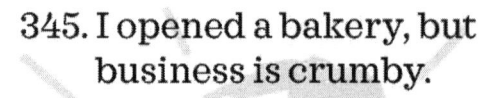

346. How do you make a lemon drop? Let it fall.

347. Why don't teddy bears ever order dessert? Because they're stuffed.

348. Why can't you trust an atom? Because they make up everything!

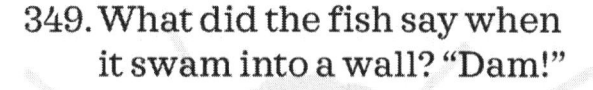

349. What did the fish say when it swam into a wall? "Dam!"

350. I tried to eat a clock yesterday, but it was too time-consuming.

351. Why don't crabs give to charity? Because they're shellfish.

352. What's a cat's favorite movie? The Sound of Mewsic.

353. Why did the dog bring a pencil to class? To do some ruff math.

354. Why did the barber win the race? Because he knew all the short cuts.

355. How does a dog stop a movie? He presses paws.

356. What's brown, hairy, and wears sunglasses? A coconut on vacation.

357. Why was the belt arrested? It was holding up a pair of pants.

358. Why was the soccer field always wet? Because the players dribbled all over it.

359. What do you call a sleeping dinosaur? A dino-snore.

360. Why don't oysters go to parties? They shell-ter at home.

361. What did the elevator say to the staircase? "I think I'm coming down with something."

362. Why did the cow become an astronaut? It wanted to see the Milky Way.

363. How do bees brush their hair? With a honeycomb.

364. Why don't lobsters share? Because they're shellfish.

365. Why did the skeleton go to the party alone? He had no body to go with him.

366. Why do mushrooms love to party? Because they're fungi.

367. Why do ducks never pay for dinner? Because their bills are always covered.

368. What did the baby corn say to the mama corn? "Where's popcorn?"

369. Why did the music teacher go to jail? Because she got caught with too many notes.

370. Why was the math book so stressed? It had too many problems.

371. Why don't teddy bears ever eat? Because they're stuffed.

372. How does a dog like his eggs? Woof-led.

373. Why don't elephants use computers? They're afraid of the mouse.

374. What's a snowman's favorite food? Icebergers.

375. What did the apple say to the orange? "You're appealing to me!"

376. How do you know carrots are good for your eyes? You never see rabbits wearing glasses.

377. What do you call a dinosaur with bad vision? A Do-you-think-he-saurus.

378. Why did the bicycle stand up by itself? It was two-tired.

379. How do cows stay up to date? They follow the moo-sletter.

380. What's the hardest part about skydiving? The ground.

381. What do you get when you cross a cow and a trampoline? A milkshake.

382. What did the buffalo say when his son left for college? "Bison."

383. Why did the calendar bring a pencil? To make a date.

384. Why do bananas never get lonely? Because they come in bunches.

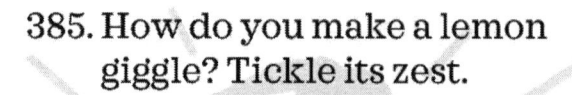

385. How do you make a lemon giggle? Tickle its zest.

386. Why don't vampires take selfies? Because they don't reflect well.

387. Why was the robot angry? It had a bad motherboard.

388. How do you make holy water? You boil the devil out of it.

389. Why do golfers bring extra socks? In case they get a hole in one.

390. Why did the cookie cry? Because its mom was a wafer so long.

391. Why don't some fish play basketball? Because they're afraid of the net.

392. What's a skeleton's least favorite room? The living room.

393. What did the blanket say to the bed? "Don't worry, I've got you covered."

394. What did one hat say to the other? "You stay here, I'll go on ahead."

395. What's a tree's favorite drink? Root beer.

396. Why don't elephants play cards in the jungle? Because of all the cheetahs.

397. What did the pencil say to the paper? "I dot my i's on you."

398. What do you call a cow with a twitch? Beef jerky.

399. What did the traffic light say to the car? "Don't look! I'm changing."

400. What do you call an angry carrot? A steamed vegetable.

401. Why did the skeleton stay out in the snow? He didn't have the guts to leave.

402. What's a computer's favorite snack? Microchips.

403. Why don't flowers play hide and seek? They're always spotted.

404. What did one plate say to another? "Lunch is on me."

405. What did the nose say to the finger? "Stop picking on me!"

406. How do you fix a broken pizza? With tomato paste.

407. What's a cat's favorite magazine? Good Mousekeeping.

408. Why don't vampires go to the beach? Because they're afraid of the sunburn.

409. Why was the broom always late? It kept sweeping in.

410. What do you call a bear in the rain? A drizzly bear.

411. What's a dog's favorite kind of pizza? Pupperoni.

412. Why did the orange stop? It ran out of juice.

413. Why did the melon jump into the lake? It wanted to be a watermelon.

414. Why did the skeleton go to the barbecue? To get a ribbing.

415. What did the candle say to the other candle? "I'm going out tonight."

416. Why can't you trust stairs? They're always up to something.

417. What's a frog's favorite exercise? Jumping jacks.

418. What did one nut say to the other? "I'm a little cracked."

419. Why did the pillow go to school? To catch some Zs.

420. Why did the horse go behind the tree? To change its hoof.

421. What's an astronaut's favorite part of a computer? The space bar.

422. What do you call a cold dog? A chili dog.

423. Why did the tree go to school? For some branching out.

424. What did the pencil say to the eraser? "You're my mistake."

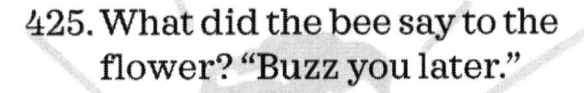

425. What did the bee say to the flower? "Buzz you later."

426. What do you call a knight with a cold? Snottingham.

427. Why did the kangaroo stop going to school? It already knew the ropes.

428. Why was the king only one foot tall? He was a ruler.

429. What do you call an elephant in a phone booth? Stuck.

430. Why don't koalas count as bears? They don't have the koalafications.

431. What's a pirate's favorite letter? "Rrr," you think, but it's the "C" they love.

432. What did the light bulb say to its partner? "You light up my life."

433. What do you get when you cross a snowman and a dog? Frostbite.

434. How do oceans say goodbye? They wave.

435. Why don't skeletons ever play music in church? They don't have any organs.

436. Why did the scarecrow become a successful stand-up comedian? He was great at corny jokes.

437. What did one volcano say to the other? "I lava you."

438. Why don't ducks ever tell jokes while flying? Because they would quack up!

439. Why did the chicken go to the gym? To work on its pecks.

440. How do you make a Kleenex dance? Put a little sneeze in it.

441. Why did the car bring a blanket? It wanted to get cozy in the garage.

442. Why did the barber win the race? He knew all the shortcuts.

443. What did the farmer say after his tractor broke down? "I'm plowing through the tough times."

444. Why do we never tell secrets in a cornfield? Too many ears around.

445. What did the belt say to the pants? "Don't worry, I've got you."

446. Why did the bread go to therapy? It had too many crumby issues.

447. Why do gorillas have big nostrils? Because they have big fingers.

448. How does a vampire start a letter? "Tomb it may concern…"

449. Why did the squirrel bring a backpack to school? To carry its nuts.

450. Why are snails so slow? Because they're carrying their house on their back!

451. Why did the cat sit on the computer? To keep an eye on the mouse.

452. Why did the belt get arrested? It was holding up a pair of pants.

453. Why don't cows play instruments? Because they're all horn and no talent.

454. Why was the soccer player a great baker? He was good at kicking rolls.

455. What do clouds wear under their clothes? Thunderwear.

456. Why was the tomato bad at racing? It couldn't ketchup.

457. Why did the dolphin get in trouble? It was blowing off steam.

458. What's a ninja's favorite type of shoes? Sneakers.

459. What's a whale's favorite music? Anything with a lot of bass.

460. What do you call a snake with a great sense of humor? Hiss-terical.

461. Why did the strawberry cry? Because it was in a jam.

462. Why did the banana join the band? Because it had a-peel.

463. Why are ghosts terrible at telling lies? Because you can see right through them.

464. Why did the chicken join the band? Because it had the drumsticks.

465. What did the policeman say to his belly button? "You're under a vest!"

466. Why did the potato become a detective? It had eyes everywhere.

467. Why was the calendar popular at school? It had a lot of dates.

468. Why was the computer tired when it got home? Because it had too many bytes during the day.

469. What did the janitor yell when he jumped out of the closet? "Supplies!"

470. What's the best way to talk to a fish? Drop it a line.

471. What did the scarf say to the hat? "You go on ahead, I'll hang around."

472. Why do cows like to go to parties? They love to moooove.

473. Why did the cow go to outer space? To visit the Milky Way.

474. What did the grape say after the elephant stepped on it? Nothing, it just let out a little whine.

475. What do you call a fish who practices medicine? A sturgeon.

476. Why did the baker go to therapy? He kneaded someone to talk to.

477. How do rabbits travel? By hare-plane.

478. Why don't skeletons ever tell scary stories? They don't have the backbone for it.

479. Why did the grape stop in the middle of the road? It ran out of juice.

480. Why was the music teacher so good at baseball? Because she had perfect pitch.

481. Why did the tree go to the dentist? It had a bad root.

482. Why do golfers love the sport? It's a hole lot of fun!

483. What did one elevator say to the other? "I think we're going up in the world."

484. Why don't giraffes go to elementary school? Because they're all in high school!

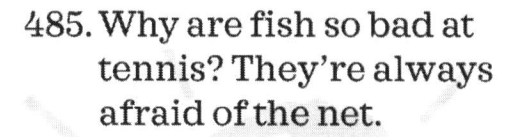

485. Why are fish so bad at tennis? They're always afraid of the net.

486. Why do ducks make good detectives? They always quack the case.

487. What do you call a bear that's stuck in the rain? A drizzly bear.

488. What did the zipper say to the jacket? "You drive me up the zip-line."

489. Why don't ants get sick? Because they have tiny ant-bodies.

490. What did the sandwich say to the cheese? "You're the best thing since sliced bread."

491. Why was the broom always late? Because it kept sweeping in and out.

492. Why are elevator jokes so funny? They always have their ups and downs.

493. What's a pig's favorite musical instrument? The ham-bone.

494. How do you turn a duck into a famous artist? Put it in a gallery!

495. Why do dogs run in circles? Because it's ruff trying to run in squares!

496. Why don't lions like fast food? Because they can't catch it.

497. How does the sun stay on schedule? It rises to the occasion.

498. Why did the golfer bring a ladder to the course? To climb up the leader board.

499. What do you get if you cross a shark and a snowman? Frostbite.

500. Why did the frog sit on a lily pad? Because it wanted a "hop-py" seat!

501. What do you call a bear that likes to paint? Pablo Pigcasso.

502. What do you call a bee that can't make up its mind? A maybee.

503. How do you get a tissue to dance? Put a little sneeze in it.

504. Why was the calendar afraid of numbers? It didn't want to date.

505. What's a skeleton's least favorite food? Spare ribs.

506. What do you call a snowman with a sunburn? A puddle.

507. Why did the turtle get detention? For coming out of his shell.

508. Why do pirates love to sing? Because they're good at keeping "arr" in tune.

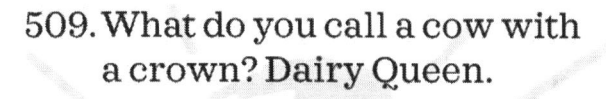

509. What do you call a cow with a crown? Dairy Queen.

510. Why did the horse go behind a tree? To change its clothes.

511. What's a duck's favorite snack? Quackers.

512. Why do elephants never use computers? They're scared of the mouse.

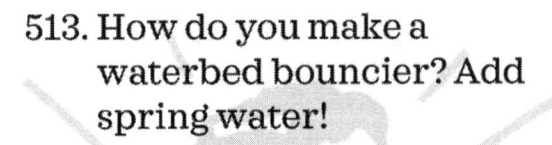

513. How do you make a waterbed bouncier? Add spring water!

514. Why did the train go to music school? It wanted to improve its tracks.

515. Why don't penguins play soccer? They're afraid of the ice.

516. What did the painter say to his girlfriend? "I love hue."

517. Why did the balloon refuse to fight? It didn't want to pop.

518. What do you call a mouse who can sing? A mice-ician.

519. Why do otters love school? Because they're always up for some fish-tional reading.

520. Why are teddy bears never hungry? They're always stuffed!

521. Why did the bird sit on the clock? Because it wanted to be on time.

522. How does a snowman lose weight? He waits until the spring!

523. Why don't spiders ever lose at hide and seek? They always spin a web of disguise.

524. Why did the baker go on vacation? He kneaded a break.

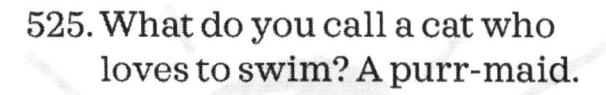

525. What do you call a cat who loves to swim? A purr-maid.

526. Why did the balloon go to therapy? It felt deflated.

527. How do you make a lemon smile? Give it a little squeeze.

528. Why did the bell get fired from the job? It couldn't stop ringing.

529. What did the watermelon say at the party? "You're one in a melon!"

530. Why don't birds use social media? They already tweet too much.

531. Why was the broom tired? It swept all night.

532. What did one wall say to the other? "I'll meet you at the corner."

533. Why don't vampires eat garlic bread? They can't handle the bite.

534. What do you get when you cross a snake and a pie? A python!

535. Why did the gardener plant a light bulb? He wanted to grow a power plant.

536. What do you call a cow in an earthquake? A milkshake!

537. Why did the music note take a break? It needed to rest.

538. What's a cow's favorite instrument? The moo-sical scale.

539. How do bees get to school? By school buzz.

540. Why was the scarecrow a great musician? He had perfect pitch.

541. What did the big candle say to the little candle? "I'm not burning out anytime soon."

542. What's a horse's favorite sport? Stable tennis.

543. Why did the banana go to the party? Because it was ripe for fun.

544. What did the cupcake say to the frosting? "You complete me!"

545. Why did the snake break up with his girlfriend? She had too much hiss-tory.

546. What do you call a group of musical whales? An orca-stra.

547. Why was the clock always late? It couldn't keep up with time.

548. Why was the ghost a bad comedian? He kept boo-ing himself.

549. Why don't apples tell secrets? They always get to the core of it.

550. What do you call a fish that loves basketball? A net-tuna.

551. Why did the cookie go to the doctor? Because it felt crummy.

552. What did the grape do when it got stepped on? It let out a little whine.

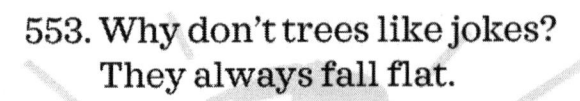

553. Why don't trees like jokes? They always fall flat.

554. What did the lemon say to the lime? "You're making me sour."

555. Why did the balloon get promoted? It really knew how to rise to the occasion.

556. What's a robot's favorite type of music? Heavy metal.

557. What did one piano say to the other? "We've got a great key-mistry."

558. Why did the toaster bring a suitcase? It was going on a toast trip.

559. What do you get when you cross a vampire with a snowstorm? Frostbite.

560. Why don't clouds ever get lost? They follow the breeze.

561. What do you call a dog that does magic? A labra-cadabra-dor.

562. Why don't refrigerators tell secrets? They can't handle the cold truth.

563. What's the most musical part of a fish? The scales.

564. Why did the pencil get detention? It wasn't sharp enough.

565. Why did the lamp break up with the candle? It found someone brighter.

566. Why do mushrooms always get invited to parties? They're such fun-guys.

567. What did the teddy bear say after dessert? "I'm stuffed!"

568. Why don't elephants write letters? They don't want to use their trunks for mail.

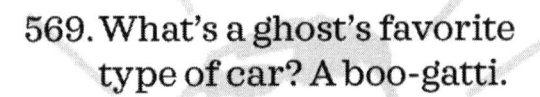

569. What's a ghost's favorite type of car? A boo-gatti.

570. Why did the beach go to school? To get its degree.

571. What do you call a cow with two legs? Lean beef.

572. How does a clock greet you? With a tick and a tock.

573. Why don't plants play poker? They're too shady.

574. What do you call a cow that can't moo? A milk dud.

575. Why do ghosts make terrible liars? You can see right through them.

576. What did the dolphin say to the whale? "You're flipping amazing!"

577. Why did the spider become a web designer? It had all the right connections.

578. How does a skeleton get around? On a skele-ton of wheels.

579. Why don't bicycles ever stand up by themselves? They're two-tired.

580. What's a snowman's favorite food? Cold cuts.

581. Why was the fish blushing? Because it saw the ocean's bottom.

582. Why do birds make terrible secret agents? They always tweet too much.

583. Why did the owl get promoted? It was a real hoot at work.

584. What's a snowman's favorite cereal? Frosted Flakes.

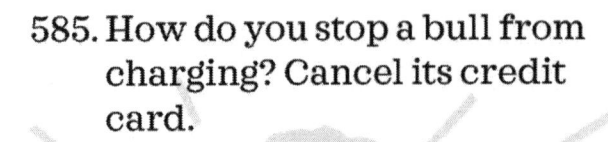

585. How do you stop a bull from charging? Cancel its credit card.

586. What's a chicken's favorite dessert? A custard crow-lar.

587. Why did the astronaut break up with his girlfriend? He needed space.

588. How do you get a baby astronaut to sleep? You rocket.

589. Why don't kangaroos make good detectives? They always jump to conclusions.

590. What's a cat's favorite color? Purr-ple.

591. Why was the clock shy? It had no time for small talk.

592. What do you call a kangaroo with no hop? A pouch potato.

593. Why do giraffes never play hide-and-seek? They're always spotted.

594. What's a vampire's favorite fruit? A blood orange.

595. Why did the frog get promoted? Because he jumped to conclusions!

596. Why did the baker stop telling jokes? He didn't want to make any more crumby puns.

597. What did the grape say when it was stepped on? "Nothing, but it let out a little whine."

598. What do you call a pony with a cough? A little horse.

599. Why don't koalas play cards? They don't like to deal.

600. Why did the frog bring a suitcase? It was going on a hop-day.

Like What You Read? Spread the Laughs!

If our jokes tickled your funny bone (or at least made you smile), we'd love to hear from you! Please take a moment to leave a review and let us know which joke had you laughing out loud—or groaning in delightful disbelief!

Whether it was the one about the talking frog or the classic suitcase in an elevator, we're all ears (and giggles) for your feedback. Your review helps keep the good times rolling!

Thanks for sharing the laughter—now, what's your favourite punchline?

Printed in Great Britain
by Amazon